CAN SCIENCE SOLVE ?

THE MYSTERY OF HAUNTED HOUSES

Chris Oxlade

Heinemann Library
Chicago, Illinois

Customer Service 888-454-2279
Visit our website at www.heinemannraintree.com

Designed by Victoria Bevan and Q2A
Printed and bound in China by WKT

10 09 08 07 06
10 9 8 7 6 5 4 3 2 1

New edition ISBNs: 1-40348-334-5 (hardcover)
                   1-40348-343-4 (paperback)

The Library of Congress has cataloged the hardcover editions as follows:
Chris Oxlade
The mystery of haunted houses / Chris Oxlade.
p. cm. - - (Can science solve?)
Includes bibliographical references and index.
Summary: Examines the phenomenon of haunted houses and their ghosts, citing
specific examples, and discusses the various theories that seek to explain them,
including how they may be faked.
        ISBN 1-57572-809-5 (lib. bdg.)   ISBN 1-58810-456-7 (pbk. bdg)
        1.   Haunted houses. [1. Haunted houses. 2. Ghosts.] I. Title.
II. Series
BF1475.W35   1999
133.1'22—dc21

                                        99-17405
                                        CIP

Acknowledgments
The author and publishers are grateful to the following for permission to
reproduce copyright material:
James David Travel Photography: p. 11 (lower); Mary Evans Picture Library:
pp. 6, 11 (upper), 15; FLPA: Silvestris p. 19; Fortean Picture Library: pp. 8, 9, 27,
A Hart-David p. 22, M Jackson p. 28, G Lyon Playfair p. 21, A Trottmann
p. 25, T Vaci p. 24; Ronald Grant Archive: p. 7; Marsden Archive: S Marsden
pp. 4, 29; Thames Water: p. 17; Trip: M Peters p. 20; Ultra Photos: Y Nixiteas
p. 23; Stewart Weir: pp. 13, 14.

Cover photograph reproduced with permission of Getty/National Geographic.

Every effort has been made to contact copyright holders of any material
reproduced in this book. Any omissions will be rectified in subsequent printings if
notice is given to the publisher.

The paper used to print this book comes from sustainable sources.

Some words are shown in bold, **like this**. You can find the definitions for these
words in the glossary.

CONTENTS

UNSOLVED MYSTERIES

For hundreds of years, people have been interested in and puzzled by mysterious places, creatures, and events. What secrets does a black hole hold? Does the Abominable Snowman actually exist? Why do ships and planes vanish without a trace when they cross the Bermuda Triangle? Are some houses really haunted by ghosts? These mysteries have baffled scientists, who have spent years trying to find the answers. But just how far can science go? Can it really explain the seemingly unexplainable? Or are there some mysteries that science simply cannot solve? Read on, and make up your own mind . . .

This book tells you about haunted houses and the ghosts in them. It retells eyewitness accounts. It looks at the possible scientific explanations for the experiences of the eyewitnesses and examines how to investigate a haunting.

Glamis Castle in Scotland is said to be haunted by many ghosts, including Macbeth, a **medieval** king. But ghosts turn up in normal houses, too.

What is a haunted house?

A ghost is said to be the soul of a dead person that returns to the world of the living. It shows its presence by appearing as a figure or a light of some kind; by making strange noises, such as clanking and laughter; or by making objects move around. A haunted house is a place where the same ghost keeps appearing, or where there are a series of ghostly events. In a haunted house, many of the ghosts that appear are in the likeness of previous occupants of the house, often ones who have met a hideous death!

It's not just houses and castles that are haunted. Any building can have a ghost—prisons, theaters, hotels, bars, and even factories.

Many stories of hauntings are made up, and many ghost sightings are just imagined. Still, there are many cases in which reliable witnesses have seen a ghost and there is no explanation. Is there anything science can do to solve this peculiar mystery?

BEGINNINGS OF A MYSTERY

It is impossible to say when people first started seeing ghosts, but it must have been many thousands of years ago. Since very ancient times, people have believed that a person's spirit can exist separately from his or her body, and that when he or she dies, the spirit lives on in some way.

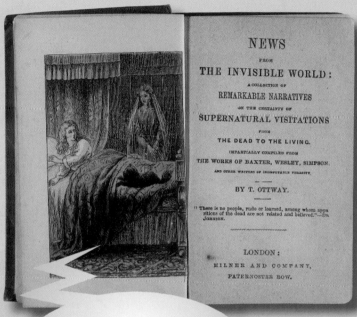

NEWS
FROM
THE INVISIBLE WORLD:
A COLLECTION OF
REMARKABLE NARRATIVES
ON THE CERTAINTY OF
SUPERNATURAL VISITATIONS
FROM
THE DEAD TO THE LIVING.
IMPARTIALLY COMPILED FROM
THE WORKS OF BAXTER, WESLEY, SIMPSON,
AND OTHER WRITERS OF INDISPUTABLE VERACITY.

BY T. OTTWAY.

"There is no people, rude or learned, among whom apparitions of the dead are not related and believed."—Dr. Johnson.

LONDON:
MILNER AND COMPANY,
PATERNOSTER ROW.

Ghost and other **paranormal** stories were popular in the 19th century, as shown by this book published in about 1850.

Ghost stories are common in **folklore**, but most are made up and exaggerated to make them as scary as possible. Over the last few hundred years, many old houses have gained a reputation for being haunted by the ghosts of people who died in them or who died on the spot where they were built. The first real investigations into hauntings were made in the 19th century.

More apparitions

Not all apparitions are haunting apparitions. Some are apparitions of the living, where people who are still alive appear to be in two places at the same time. "Crisis" apparitions have appeared when a living person dies or is involved in an accident. They normally appear to the victim's friend or relative, who is in a completely different place. Some apparitions are not hauntings, because they appear only once.

Types of ghost

When you think of a ghost, you probably think of a Hollywood movie ghost: a **transparent** figure dressed in white, floating through the walls of an old house and making strange moaning noises! In fact, there are very few sightings of ghosts like this.

A ghost can be in the form of an **apparition**, which is a visible figure of a person. An apparition might look solid or transparent, float through the air, or walk. Apparitions are not always of people—they are sometimes of animals or monsters. The apparition can be accompanied by noises.

Not all hauntings involve an apparition. Often there are just noises such as laughter, music, footsteps, groaning, or whistling, and some hauntings involve objects that appear to move on their own. This sort of ghost is called a **poltergeist**. A poltergeist is normally, but not always, **malicious**, throwing objects across rooms, stones against windows, overturning furniture, and so on. The word *poltergeist* means "noisy spirit."

This is the apparition of Marley's ghost from the 1970 version of the movie *Scrooge*—with clanking chains for effect!

DID YOU SEE THAT?

There are literally thousands of people who have had ghostly experiences in haunted houses and other buildings. Obviously we cannot look at them all in this book. So, on the next four pages, we will look at examples that show the range of experiences people have had in haunted houses. We'll start with an in-depth look at one of the most famous haunted houses ever.

Borley Rectory

For more than a century, Borley **Rectory**, a 19th-century building in Borley, England, was famous as one of the world's most haunted houses. Borley Rectory was built in 1863, close to Borley Church and on ground where a **medieval** monastery had once stood.

The rectory's first residents were the Reverend Henry Bull and his family. Not long after moving in, they began to hear footsteps, tapping noises, voices, and ringing bells at night. Then, ghostly figures began to appear; one child saw an old man in a hat at her bedside and a visitor saw a nun wandering in the hallways.

This is Borley Rectory, in 1929.

In 1892 Henry Bull's son took over the rectory, but the strange happenings continued. The residents saw a headless man in the garden and a ghostly carriage in the driveway. A locked door mysteriously unlocked itself every night. In 1929 **poltergeists** moved in. Keys and other objects began to appear from nowhere. Later, new occupants heard voices and footsteps and saw scribbled messages appear on the walls.

These are some of the scrawled messages that appeared mysteriously on the walls of Borley Rectory. (The capital letters were written by investigators.)

The bizarre events continued until 1939, when the rectory was mysteriously burned to the ground. Witnesses saw dark figures leaving the burning building and a young girl's face looking from one of the upstairs windows, even though there should have been nobody inside.

Eventually, houses were built on the site. Nobody knows the reasons for the hauntings, but as workers dug into the ground to build the new houses, pendants (ornaments for necklaces) with religious symbols were found, together with a woman's skull. There is also a theory that the ghosts were of a monk from the former monastery and a nun from a nearby convent, who were killed as they tried to run away together in a carriage with horses.

MORE HAUNTINGS

Here are four other cases of hauntings, which have been chosen to show the wide range of different ghostly experiences that people have had in haunted houses.

New Orleans nursery

An elegant home in New Orleans, Louisiana, has seldom been lived in since the 1860s after the housekeeper gave birth to a deformed baby. The child died shortly after it was born and was secretly buried within the nursery walls. The baby's mother died soon after of a fever. But, witnesses said the young mother still roamed the house.

When the house was repainted many years later, the painter could not cover a large, black patch on the nursery wall, so a frame picture was hung over it. The artwork did not stay up for long. One night, after a large crash, the picture was found torn off the wall and thrown across the room.

The Octagon of Washingtom, D.C.

The word octagon means eight-sided, but the house called the Octagon in Washington, D.C. has only six sides. No one knows why. One of the Octagon's most colorful ghost stories is about Dolley Madison, the wife of President James Madison. After the War of 1812, Dolley held many parties while living in the Octagon. Years later guests at the Octagon said they heard voices of unseen party-goers. Some believe Dolley is still enjoying a party in the ballroom.

The White House, the official residence of the president of the United States, is said to be haunted by the ghost of Abraham Lincoln, who was president from 1861 to 1865.

Cottage poltergeist

In 1878, in Nova Scotia, Canada, 19-year-old Esther woke up screaming, "What's wrong with me? I'm dying." Her face and arms were swollen and painful. Knocking sounds were heard throughout the house.

Esther's **poltergeist**, whom she called Bob, scratched threatening messages to her on walls and played with matches. When Esther worked at a restaurant, chairs fell over and dishes broke. Esther lost her job. Later she was imprisoned for burning down a barn. Esther blamed the poltergeist, but the judge did not believe her.

Manse of Major Weir

The Weir house was once the most haunted house in Edinburgh, Scotland. In 1670, Major Thomas Weir, an honest and religious man, confessed to witchcraft. He was hanged. After his execution, people reported strange lights and sounds of dancing and howling coming from his empty house.

BUMPS IN THE NIGHT

Most reports of hauntings involve strange noises rather than **apparitions**. The wide range of sounds that witnesses hear includes creaking, bumps, cracks, knocks, sliding noises, groaning, laughter, and crying. Can any of these ghostly noises be explained by science?

Expansion and contraction

All materials expand (get bigger) and contract (get smaller) when their temperature changes. In most cases, they expand as the temperature rises and contract as the temperature falls. The amount that a material expands or contracts is very small. For example, a wooden yardstick would only expand by a fraction of a millimeter if its temperature increased by 1.8 °F (1 °C).

Different materials expand and contract at different rates, so the expansion of one material might be greater than the expansion of another if they both undergo the same temperature rise. If two materials that expand and contract at different rates are pressed against each other, then as the temperature rises and falls, they try to move against each other. Because of **friction**, the movement does not happen smoothly, but in a series of little jumps. As each jump happens, the materials vibrate, creating a knocking noise, or a creaking noise if the jumps happen quickly in a row.

If you have central heating in your home, you might hear creaking noises as the heating comes on and the pipes and radiators begin to warm up. It is caused by the metal pipes expanding and moving against their fastenings.

Wood does not necessarily have to be in contact with other materials to make creaking noises. Wood is made of millions of fibers lying next to each other, so if some fibers expand before the fibers next to them, creaking noises can result. The expansion can be caused by heating and cooling, but also if the wood becomes damp or dries out. Water makes its way into the fibers and makes them expand. The **water vapor** in damp air is enough to make the outer layers of the wood expand.

This old doorway contains a combination of materials—iron, wood, and brick —that expand and contract at different rates.

WEATHER CHANGES

The changes of temperature and **humidity** that cause building materials to make creaking noises are regularly created by the weather. On a sunny morning, sunshine hits a cold building. Dark parts of the building capture the heat and warm up. At the end of the day, as the Sun goes down and the air cools, so does the building, with the outside parts cooling first. These regular changes, especially the ones at night, can be the cause of ghostly noises. Also, as the weather patterns or seasons change and bring changes of humidity, dry wood can gradually become damp and vice versa.

Renovations

Alterations and additions to a building also create the conditions that cause its structure and furnishings to creak. For example, putting a central heating system into an old house makes the lumber of the house, which may have been slightly damp for hundreds of years, gradually dry out. Installing new windows and doors, which create new air flows through the house, or uncovering beams to give the house an old-fashioned look can also cause lumber to dry out.

Old houses such as this have wooden frames, which dry out and creak if modern heating is installed.

Expansion and contraction of new window and door frames can cause not only creaking, but also the windows and doors themselves to jam closed and even to open by themselves.

Plumbing

Plumbing, especially old plumbing, also causes strange noises. Air trapped in the pipes causes peculiar gurgling noises as the water flows past it. Sound also travels very well along the pipes, so a sound made in one place can seem to come from everywhere in the house. Water hammer, which is caused by shock **waves** bouncing from one end of a pipe to the other if a faucet is closed too quickly, creates very loud clanking noises.

So, it may not be a coincidence that older houses, which tend to have a wooden framework of columns and beams as well as old plumbing, seem more likely to be haunted by ghostly noises.

Plumbing installed in the 19th century is often a cause of ghostly glugs and gurgles!

SOUND ON THE MOVE

One reason why noises sound ghostly is that they often seem to come out of thin air. For example, you might hear the sound of talking from an empty room. Many such occurrences can be explained by investigating the way in which sound travels.

Waves and echoes

Sound is created by any object that vibrates. The vibrations travel away from the object in **waves**. As the sound travels, it gets weaker, so the farther away a listener is from you, the quieter your voice sounds. When sound hits the boundary between two different materials, it bounces.

In fact, sound does not travel very well in air. It travels much better through solids and liquids. So, imagine if a person taps a plumbing pipe in one room of a house. Sound waves go both into the air and into the pipe. In the air, the sound weakens and bounces off the walls. But in the pipe, it travels well through the solid metal and can be heard clearly in all the other rooms in the house where the plumbing goes. The same thing happens with solid walls and floors: sound travels easily from room to room and even from house to house.

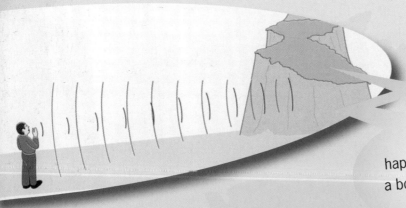

Ghostly echoes happen when sound reaches a boundary in materials, such as the air or rock.

Sounds under the ground

Underground mine shafts and tunnels may be the cause of haunting effects. Sound travels along them, making sounds from far off seem to come from the ground, and air moves through them, making them behave like a huge musical instrument. Sounds traveling down into the ground, such as footsteps, can also be reflected back up when they hit the tunnels. Other **geological** features, such as the boundary between layers of soft and hard rock, can reflect sound, and hidden underground streams and water pipes carry sound well.

Ground subsidence

Subsidence happens when the ground collapses under a building's foundations. It is caused by old mine workings collapsing or soft rocks such as clay drying out in a dry summer. Subsidence sometimes causes a disaster, but normally it happens slowly, with the building slowly cracking. As the ground and foundations move, the house will make creaking and cracking noises without the movements being felt inside.

Underground tunnels, such as this sewer, can cause unusual sounds and echoes.

NOT WHAT IT SEEMS

We've seen how most ghostly sounds can be explained as creaks and groans made by the houses that are supposed to be haunted. But what can science do to explain **apparitions** and objects moving around on their own?

Tricks of the light

At night in a spooky house, it's easy to imagine shadows and lights as ghostly figures. However, a trick of the light can be the cause. For example, the glass in old windows is never perfectly flat because of the way it was made. Light does not pass straight through, but is **refracted** in different directions, distorting the images of objects on the other side. Simple reflections, even of yourself, in glass doors can also look like ghostly figures because the glass creates a **transparent** reflection. You don't normally notice these reflections because of the light coming from the other side of the glass.

Light can also be reflected from outside the house. For example, light from car headlights can shine from a long distance through windows and be reflected around, creating ghostly images. On stormy nights, lightning can create similar effects. Outside, especially in marshy (soft, wet) ground, small patches of rising mist can look like ghostly figures.

Fog and mist, such as this early morning mist over a lake, can make the shapes of common objects look like ghostly figures.

Moving objects

The same ground movements that cause houses to **subside** can also cause objects in the house to move around. Gradual, slow movement over a period of days may go unnoticed, but can cause shelves and surfaces to slope slightly over time. Sometimes the overall movement is enough to make objects slide or topple as if they are being moved by an invisible hand.

Low-frequency noise

The **frequency** of a sound is a measure of how many **waves** pass a point every second. It is measured in hertz. The human ear can detect a wide range of frequencies, but not very high or very low ones. Research has shown that very low-frequency noise (lower than 10 hertz) can cause some people to "see" objects that are not really there, perhaps because the sound vibrates the eye's **retina** in some way.

19

ALL IN THE MIND

Apparitions are hard to explain. If the witnesses are reliable and the apparition cannot be simply explained as a trick of the light, then there seems to be no logical explanation for why they see a ghostly figure. Unless, that is, the apparition is a trick of the mind—a **hallucination** of some sort.

Hallucinations are a recognized medical side-effect. Diseases such as malaria can make people hallucinate, and so can taking certain medications for treating disease. Of course, we all have hallucinations when we dream, and it's likely that many "ghosts" simply appear in very realistic dreams. However, simple hallucinations would not seem to explain ghosts that are seen by several people at the same time.

Clairvoyants use their natural "sixth sense," or ESP, to see into the future. Some people are convinced it works; others are doubtful.

Other theories about hallucinations rely on the existence of extra-sensory perception (ESP). This is where a person somehow receives information in his or her brain without using the normal five senses (sight, hearing, smell, taste, touch) to collect it. The theories suggest that the person who sees the ghost actually sees a picture projected into his or her mind by somebody else. Scientific experiments have been carried out to try to show that ESP exists, but none have been conclusive.

Back from the dead

Parapsychologists believe that dead people's spirits live on and can affect living people. The dead people may use ESP to project their presence into a living person's mind, so that the living person sees them, perhaps on purpose, perhaps by mistake. Parapsychologists believe that some people have a natural ability to pick up these signals from the dead, and the signals are from dead people telling the living that death is not the end of life, or that they are refusing to accept their own death.

Mind over matter

Telekinesis is the ability of a person to make objects move without touching them, using mind power alone. Some parapsychologists think that **poltergeists** are spirits using telekinesis. Again, experiments have been carried out to see if telekinesis is possible, such as a person trying to affect the roll of dice, but none have been conclusive.

Paranormalist
Uri Geller bends a spoon, apparently by mind power alone. Could the spirits of the dead move objects in a similar way?

21

HAUNTED HOUSE INVESTIGATIONS

To attempt to discover the possible cause of a haunting, it is necessary to carry out a special investigation of the haunted site. Psychic investigators specialize in these investigations. An investigation needs a logical, scientific approach to find the facts of the case, to discover a natural cause if there is one, and to rule out other causes.

The witnesses

An investigator's first job is to interview the witnesses who have seen or heard anything and to write down, or record on tape, what they say. The interview includes asking questions that attempt to find out what actually happened rather than the witness' interpretation of what happened. For example, the witness may say that he or she heard footsteps. It is up to an investigator to find out what the "footsteps" really sounded like, because it may have been different from his or her idea of what footsteps sound like. Questions like this can also help the investigator to decide whether the witness' story is reliable, exaggerated, or even invented.

Researchers record ground vibrations caused by underground water movements, which they think could cause objects to move in a "haunted" house.

The investigator should also ask about the witnesses' health and whether they are taking medications, because illness and drugs can cause **hallucinations** or affect sight.

The haunted site

The investigator should also take a close examination of the haunted site. This includes making an accurate plan (drawing) of the rooms where the witness saw or heard the ghost. The plan should include the positions of the witnesses and the movements of the **apparition** or the direction any sounds appeared to come from. They should also note the position of anything that could affect the light or sound in the rooms, such as windows, mirrors, and thin walls. Photographs of the rooms can also be taken to go with the plan.

Armed with the statements, recordings, plans, photographs, and notes, an investigator can go away and attempt to solve the mystery, perhaps with the help of old maps and books on local history. He or she may be able to suggest a natural cause, such as faulty plumbing, but there will not always be an explanation.

HAUNTED HOUSE STAKEOUT

After investigating a haunting, a **psychic investigator** may want to wait at the site in an attempt to see or hear the ghost for him or herself. This requires an approach just as scientific as the initial investigation, but more than anything, it requires patience!

Tools of the trade

Certain pieces of equipment are essential for ghost hunting, and others are useful. Basic tools are a notebook and pens, a flashlight, a tape measure for making plans of rooms, a tape recorder, and a camera. Compact cameras, digital cameras, and video cameras are all suitable. The important thing is that a camera can often pick up low-light details that the naked eye cannot.

The trickiest part of ghost hunting is finding the ghosts in the first place, before you can photograph them. Investigators use several scientific instruments that show changes in the conditions in an area that may not be visible to the naked eye. These changes may indicate something peculiar going on, which may be linked to ghostly happenings. Unfortunately, there are still no convincing scientific links between these physical changes and what people see.

Patience can sometimes be rewarded! This photograph, taken in 1974 in a cemetery in Chicago, reveals a mysterious mist.

Measuring temperature

Psychic investigators often report a drop in temperature during apparent ghostly activity. A simple room thermometer will measure temperature, but a better device is an **infrared,** non-contact thermometer. This detects the strength of infrared rays coming from an object. All objects give off infrared rays, and the hotter the object, the more rays it gives off. The non-contact thermometer shows the temperature of anything it is pointed at.

Magnetic fields

Ghost hunters have also found that ghostly events are often accompanied by a **magnetic field**, just like the magnetic field around an **electromagnet**. So, they carry a device called an electromagnetic field (EMF) meter, which measures the strength of the magnetic field it is in.

Thermometers and EMF meters can be electronically linked to a camera so that the camera automatically takes a picture when the temperature or magnetic field changes. This sounds useful, but deciding where to point the camera is a problem, since nobody knows where the ghost will appear.

This house in Switzerland has been the scene of many strange happenings, from rattling chains and voices to **apparitions** and moving objects.

FAKES AND PHOTOS

There is no doubt that some hauntings are faked. There are numerous reasons for claiming to have a ghost in your house. For a start, people like ghosts and ghost stories. If you owned a very old house that was open to the public to visit, imagine how many more visitors you would get if you promised to show them where the ghost of a long-dead, murdered person is regularly seen! It could be tempting to fake the haunting—after all, nobody could prove you hadn't seen it. Now, you can see why owners of old houses, hotels, bars, and restaurants play up stories of ghosts rather than try to keep them quiet. They may even gain publicity by appearing in the local papers, on television, and on the radio. They might be able to write books to sell. Of course, there is strong competition to claim the title of "most haunted house."

Other reasons for fake hauntings include children's pranks to frighten grown-ups on Halloween, attempts to encourage people to go on haunted house guided tours, and even attempts to frighten people out of their houses.

Theater ghosts

Many famous theaters are said to be haunted. Through stage tricks, at least, ghostly figures can appear on stage during plays. This is done by having a sheet of glass on the stage that reflects the light from a hidden actor.

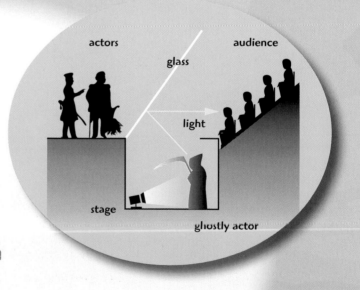

This famous photograph of a ghostly figure was taken at Raynham Hall, Norfolk, England, in 1936. It was probably faked by taking two photographs from the same spot.

Photographs of ghosts

People are most intrigued by spectacular ghosts, such as long-dead soldiers with clanking armor or vicious **poltergeists**. Apart from actually seeing the ghost, the best evidence would be a photograph of a ghostly figure or a floating armchair. Fake photographs are easy to put together, especially with modern computer graphics and **digital photography**. There are several old photographs that are claimed to show ghosts, but they were taken by accident rather than on purpose. Close inspection and computer enhancement shows that they are probably multiple photographs, created by two photographs being **superimposed** because the film did not wind correctly.

WHAT DO YOU THINK?

So, can science really solve the mystery of haunted houses? The lack of solid and reliable scientific evidence probably means the answer is, "No—not at the moment." Remember that investigators have visited many haunted houses, but have found no conclusive proof that ghosts exist. Proving that they don't exist is impossible.

Do theories about sound, light, and moving ground provide any answers?

Sounds convincing . . .
- Materials expanding and contracting as they get hotter or colder can cause creaks and bumps, especially in old buildings.

- There are lots of old tunnels and mines underground, which can make the ground move, which causes doors to open by themselves and things to fall off shelves.

- Glass in old windows is rarely flat and can cause strange tricks of the light.

But what about . . . ?
- Ghost stories have existed for thousands of years. Can they all be explained by strange sounds in old buildings?

- Psychic investigators have also found strange magnetic fields where ghostly events have been reported.

- How can we explain the detailed eyewitness reports of ghosts?

Trick or truth? This photograph shows a two-year-old boy looking at the ghost of his great-grandmother.

Would you go to this spooky graveyard at night?

There's no doubt that the science of light and sound can explain many odd sights and noises. But, if witnesses are to be believed—and we must assume that they are not all making up or exaggerating their experiences—then there are some hauntings that science cannot explain.

What about the other theories? Do you think any of them might be true? Look at the list of theories below and think about the pros and cons of each. Decide which you think are the most convincing.

- Low-**frequency** sounds that are not heard by the human ear can cause people to see things that aren't really there.

- **Hallucinations** are a side-effect of diseases like malaria.

- Some people have a natural ability to pick up signals from the dead by extra-sensory perception (ESP).

- Ghost stories and photos are all fakes.

What are your conclusions? Are there theories you can dismiss without further investigation? Do you have any theories of your own? Perhaps you believe that the spirit lives on after death, in which case ghosts may not seem so strange to you. Try to keep an open mind. Remember that science is constantly evolving and new discoveries are being made all the time. Just because something can't be proved scientifically now, it doesn't mean this will always be the case.

GLOSSARY

apparition visible figure of a person that is not really the person him or herself

digital photography photography with a digital camera that records pictures electronically as data instead of chemically on film. The pictures can be loaded into a computer.

electromagnet magnet made when an electric current flows through a coil of wire

folklore traditional stories and beliefs of a group of people

frequency number of times an event happens. The frequency of a wave is the number of wave crests that pass a point every second.

friction force between two surfaces that tries to stop the surfaces from sliding against each other. The more the surfaces are pressed together, the larger the force of friction is.

geological to do with the structure of Earth or the pattern and types of rocks under the ground

hallucination when you think you see or hear something that is not really there

humidity amount of water vapor (the gas form of water) in the air. The air is very humid on a hot, sticky day.

infrared type of ray similar to light, but that is invisible to the human eye and carries heat away from where it is made. For example, a fire gives out infrared rays that you feel as heat on your skin.

magnetic field region around a magnet (or electromagnet) where its magnetic force can be felt

malicious with the intention to do harm

medieval from a period of European history dating from C.E. 500 to 1500

paranormal describes anything that cannot be explained by scientific investigation. Those who study the paranormal are called paranormalists.

parapsychologist person who studies events that cannot be explained by present-day science, such as extra-sensory perception (ESP)

poltergeist type of ghost that makes noises and moves objects, but is never seen

psychic relating to the supernatural

rectory residence of a church leader

refracted light is refracted, or bent, when it passes through different substances, such as water

retina layer of cells at the back of an eye that detects the brightness and color of the light that hits it and sends messages to the brain

subsidence when underground rocks settle or collapse, making the surface sink downward. Subsidence can damage buildings.

superimposed placed on top of something else

telekinesis apparent movement of objects without anyone or anything touching them

transparent see-through, or allowing light to pass through it

water vapor gas form of water, formed when water boils. It is always present in the air.

wave movement in a substance, such as water or air, that passes through the substance, carrying energy with it. For example, a sound wave is made up of a compression traveling through the air.

Find Out More

You can find out more about haunted houses in books and on the Internet. Use a search engine such as www.yahooligans.com to search for information. A search for the words "haunted house" will bring back lots of results, but it may be difficult to find the information you want. Try narrowing your search to look for some of the people and ideas mentioned in this book, such as "Abraham Lincoln ghost" or "parapsychology."

More Books to Read

Cohen, Daniel. *Real Ghosts*. New York: Sagebrush, 1999.

Townsend, John. *Out There? Mysterious Visitors*. Chicago: Heinemann Library, 2004.

INDEX